Writing Degree Zero

P9-AFO-293

Camera Lucida
new Critical Essays

Writing
Degree Zero

Roland
Barthes

Preface by SUSAN SONTAG
Translated from the French by
Annette Lavers and Colin Smith

 HILL AND WANG • NEW YORK
A DIVISION OF FARRAR, STRAUS AND GIROUX

Translated from the French *Le Degré Zéro de L'Ecriture*
© 1953 by Editions du Seuil
Translation © 1967 by Jonathan Cape Ltd.
Preface copyright © 1968 by Susan Sontag
All rights reserved
Library of Congress catalog card number: 68-14789
Manufactured in the United States of America
First American edition, March 1968
Fifth printing, 1980

Contents

PREFACE

To describe Barthes as a literary critic does him an obvious injustice. A man of prodigious learning, unflagging mental energy, and acutely original sensibility, he has established his credentials as aesthetician, literary and theatre critic, sociologist, metapsychologist, social critic, historian of ideas, and cultural journalist. Only if the ideal of criticism is enlarged to take in a wide variety of discourse, both theoretical and descriptive, about culture, language, and contemporary consciousness, can Barthes plausibly be called a critic. Karl Kraus, T. W. Adorno, and Kenneth Burke come to mind as other distinguished examples of this rare breed of intellectual virtuoso, while McLuhan suggests the risks of radical unevenness of quality and judgment incurred with this magnitude of intellectual appetite and ambition. Evaluation at this virtually unclassifiable level of achievement may seem somewhat frivolous. Still, I would argue that Barthes is the most consistently intelligent, important, and useful critic —stretching that term—to have emerged anywhere in the last fifteen years.

Writing Degree Zero, long overdue in English translation, is Barthes' first book; it appeared in 1953. Seen from the perspective of 1968, however, *Writing Degree Zero* probably isn't the easiest text with which to start an acquaintance with Barthes. The book is compact to the point of ellipsis, often arcane. It barely suggests the variety and intellectual mobility of Barthes' subsequent work —which now totals six books, only one of which has already been brought out in the United States,* and numerous uncollected essays. Though explicitly theoretical in character, the argument here can't compare in rigor or completeness with Barthes' later development of some of these ideas in his "Eléments de Sémiologie," the systematic treatise first published in issue No. 4 (1964) of *Communications,* the important French journal of which he is an editor. Moreover, *Writing Degree Zero* gives virtually no indication of Barthes' sensitivity and imaginativeness in handling individual literary texts and and in stating the unifying metaphors of a single author's body of work, skills he was to exercise in the short book on Michelet (1954) and in the influential studies of Brecht and Robbe-Grillet written in the mid 1950's. Lastly, the present text doesn't disclose the witty concreteness of Barthes' sensibility, his talent for sensuous phenomenological description, evidenced in the brilliant essay-epiphanies collected in 1957 under the title *Mythologies.* Thus, *Writing Degree Zero* is early Barthes, seminal but not representative. (Perhaps only the collection published in 1964, *Essais Critiques,* spanning work from 1953 to 1963, gives in one book anything like a reasonable sample of Barthes' range.) And, even apart from this proviso, the book may present considerable difficulties to the reader unacquainted with the background and provenance of Barthes' argument.

Sur Racine (1963) was published by Hill and Wang in 1964 as *On Racine,* in a translation by Richard Howard.

Writing Degree Zero must be located in the context of a cultural situation in two important respects unlike our own.

First, Barthes is addressing a literary community which has for several generations, on most levels, honored and treated as central a canon of contemporary work still regarded as marginal and suspect by the Anglo-American literary community. Such "difficult" literary tendencies as Symbolism and Surrealism, and in particular the line of post-novel prose narrative from the Surrealist fictions to those of Borges, Beckett, and Robbe-Grillet, are taken to occupy the central position in contemporary letters — while most novels in traditional "realistic" forms (such as continue to this day to be *critical* successes in England and America) are regarded as essentially uninteresting, barely noteworthy products of a retarded or reactionary consciousness. Inevitably, this triumph of literary "modernism" in Paris has had its impact on critical debate, shifting the substantive concerns and the tone of serious literary discussion. In this country, of course, a quite different taste prevails, and comparable work — from late Joyce, Stein, and late Virginia Woolf to Burroughs — is still generally regarded as a provocative minority current, labeled "avant-garde" or "experimental" literature. (The critical situation that *is* comparable here is the consensus of "avant-garde" standards for painting which have prevailed ever since the early 1950's, with the consecration by both the art-world elite and Time-Life style popularizers of Pollock, DeKooning, Kline, Motherwell, Rothko, *et al.*)

Second, Barthes' book is a late contribution to that vigorous debate that has engaged the European literary community since the decade before the war on the relation between politics and literature. No debate of similar quality on that topic ever took place here. Despite all rumors that there once existed a generation of politically radical writers in England and America, the question of the political-ethical responsibility of writers was never posed here in anything better than an embryonic, intellectually crude form—a lone exception being the brilliant books published in the late 1930's by the young Christopher Caudwell.

It's against this background that *Writing Degree Zero* must be situated. Because Barthes is addressing a sizable literary community at home in and respectful of literary modernism, most of which has accepted some variety of left-wing or neo-Marxist political stance—both conditions, especially the former, being quite untypical of the literary community in the English-speaking world—he simply takes for granted a great deal that we do not. *Writing Degree Zero* lends support to the already well-established cause of advanced literature, not with an argument over fundamentals of taste and purpose, but by an allusive refinement of that argument, oriented more to modernist literature's further prospects than to its celebrated past. But *Writing Degree Zero* is not only manifesto but polemic. With any difficult text, the reader, in order to understand what the philosopher or critic is arguing *for*, must grasp what or whom he is tacitly arguing *against*. Considered as a polemic, Barthes is challenging the most intelligent version of the theory of literature's obligation to be socially committed, that theory having always entailed some attack, overt or implicit, on the tradition of modernist literature.

Indeed, I think, one can name the specific adversary of Barthes' argument. Barthes' topic is the same as that posed by, and stated in the title of, Sartre's famous *What Is Literature?* (Supplementary confirmation by dates:

although *Writing Degree Zero* was published in 1953, early portions of it appeared in the newspaper *Combat* in 1947, the same year Sartre's book was published. And both Sartre's first chapter and the first section of *Writing Degree Zero* have the same title: ("What Is Writing?"). It would seem that Barthes, though he never mentions Sartre's book, had it in mind when he wrote *Writing Degree Zero*, and that his argument constitutes an attempt at refuting Sartre's. Where *What Is Literature?* is prolix (but easily readable) and contains extended passages of powerful, concrete historical and psychological analysis of the writer's situation and of postwar society, *Writing Degree Zero* is terse and unconcrete (and rather difficult of access)—as if Barthes were depending on his reader's familiarity with the generous development of the terms of the debate provided by Sartre.

Sartre takes the position, already advanced for different purposes by Valéry, that prose literature differs from all the other arts, by virtue of its means—language. Words, unlike images, signify; they convey meaning. Therefore, prose literature by its nature is bound, as is no other art, including poetry, to the task of communicating. The writer is (potentially) a giver of consciousness, a liberator. His medium, language, confers on him an ethical obligation: to aid in the project of bringing liberty to *all* men—and this ethical criterion must be the foundation of any sound literary judgment. Thus Sartre's inquiry into the nature of literature is throughout governed by this ethical conception of the writer's vocation, as is his relatively pejorative treatment of the "crisis of language which broke out at the beginning of this century," which he characterizes as a situation favoring the production of private, obscurantist literary art works confined to "an audience of specialists." Believing that "literature is in essence a taking of positions," Sartre argues that "art has never been on the side of the purists."

Disregarding much of the feast of argument in Sartre's brilliant book, Barthes' thesis in *Writing Degree Zero* confronts only this basic view of literature by which Sartre supports his theory of the writer's "engagement." Sartre begins by distinguishing *language*, whose "end" or function is to communicate, from *style*, understood as the most efficient means of expressing the "subject," of putting down something. Language is the collective inventory, what is given to the writer; style is what is chosen, the "how" one renders "what one wants to write about." In refutation, Barthes offers a subtler set of categories. Instead of the common-sense dualism of language (social property) and style (individual decision), Barthes proposes the triad of language, style, and "writing." (These he calls the three dimensions of "form." Compare Sartre's astonishingly naive statement: "There is nothing to be said about form in advance, and we have said nothing. Everyone invents his own, and one judges it afterward.")

Thus Barthes begins with an account of language, one in essential agreement with Sartre's. Language, whose function is communication, is both "a social object" and "a kind of natural ambiance," the writer's "horizon," his "field of action," something that "enfolds the whole of literary creation" without endowing it with any specific form or content. All of history stands behind language — history "unified and complete in the manner of a natural order." Barthes was to adopt a different and far more complex view of language in later books — when he came under the successive influence of Saussurian linguistics, then of the ahistorical methods of "structural" analysis developed by Jakobson and Lévi-Strauss, and, most recently, of the account of the relation of language and the unconscious expounded by Lacan. But in this first book, it is only when Barthes treats the second of Sartre's pair of terms, style, that the difference made by having added a third term shows up.

By style Barthes means something quite different from the servant of content (as Sartre would have it). Its frame of reference is not historical, like language's, but "biological or biographical." Style is "indifferent to society," a closed "personal process." In its origin "the transmutation of a humour," style "is never anything but metaphor." Therefore, in Barthes' conceptual geography, style resides "outside art" (since it is "outside the pact that binds the writer to society") just as much as language does. If language stands on the "hither side of literature," style is located beyond it.

What remains for Barthes is the task of identifying what is peculiar to (or inside) literature, something that has to be distinct from both language and style. For this third term Barthes uses *écriture*, which may cause English-language readers difficulty. To translate *écriture* as "writing" is literally correct, but Barthes' meaning relies on a special inflection of the French word that has no equivalent in the English "writing." (Once we had the word "scripture," but that's no longer available.) A more helpful translation of what Barthes means by *écriture* — the ensemble of features of a literary work such as tone, ethos, rhythm of delivery, naturalness of expression, atmosphere of happiness or malaise — might be "personal utterance." For Barthes a language and a style are "objects," while a mode of *écriture* (writing, personal utterance) is a "function." Neither strictly historical nor irredeemably personal, *écriture* occupies a middle ground; it is "essentially the morality of form." In contrast to a language and a style, *écriture* is the writer's zone of freedom, "form considered as human intention."

It should be evident that Barthes' reply to Sartre hardly reasserts a doctrine of literature for literature's sake. Barthes isn't claiming that literature does or should exist in a social, historical, or ethical vacuum. As Barthes says, every given mode of *écriture* owes its existence to "the writer's consideration of the social use which he has chosen for his form and his committment to this choice." But literature, conceived as an instrumentality, cannot be confined to its social or ethical context. Insisting on the implications of Sartre's Kantian conception of the writer as the guardian of ideal "ends," Barthes suggests that Sartre has suppressed the fact that the choices made by writers always face in *two* directions: toward society and toward the nature of literature itself. Though the choice of a given manner of *écriture* amounts to "the choice of that social area within which the writer elects to situate the nature of his language," the writer can't place literature at the service of a social group or ethical end (as Sartre implies), deciding matters of "actual consumption." The writer's choice—which amounts to "a way of conceiving literature"—is a matter of "conscience, not of efficacy."

What Barthes is trying to allow is a more complex view of literature—a view of literature freed from the simplifications imposed by yielding to ethical euphoria, innocent of the necessity of "judgment." In many ways, of course, Barthes is close to Sartre's ethical and political position of that time—the values of "freedom," the contempt for the impasses of bourgeois culture, the horizon of the Revolution. What most profoundly separates them is their capacity for the moralistic judgment, so that Barthes can go a certain way with all of Sartre's arguments but must stop well short of their final crystal-lization—as when Sartre suggests that modernist litera-ture (with its accelerating fragmentation of personal utterance) embodies the final cop-out of "bourgeois consciousness," a default which can be reversed only by the ascendancy of a new, "revolutionary consciousness." Barthes at that time was perfectly capable of using this fairly crude left-Hegelian rhetoric—a good part of the later argument of his book relies on the distinction be-tween "classical language" and "bourgeois language"—and would have agreed, probably still agrees, with most of the ingredients that enter into this diagnosis, such as the view that literature is passing through the most pro-found and desperate crisis of its language and means. Still, Barthes could never end with so flat a judgment. For instance, he is disinclined to attribute bad faith or moral delinquency to the great writers from Flaubert forward who have erected literature into a fundamentally *problematic* activity. (Indeed, as he points out, it's only recently that literature, strictly speaking, comes into existence—as a problem.) Further, Barthes is skeptical—rightly, I think—of the solution Sartre envisages. As he says, "There is no writing which can be lastingly revo-lutionary." (Scathing judgment *is* reserved—this is 1953 —about the way most Communist writers employ a language steeped in conventionality, presenting "reality in a prejudged form" and thereby perpetuating "a bour-geois writing which bourgeois writers have themselves condemned long ago." Barthes remarks that the writing typical of all authoritarian regimes always seeks to pro-mote "order," i.e. repression.)

Thus, while Barthes' austere, aphoristic book lacks anything comparable to the eloquence and noble passion of the long passages of moral exhortation in *What Is*

Literature? (particularly the chapter "Why Write?"), it should be remembered with what simplifications of the issue Sartre has paid for the ethical elevation of his argument. Barthes, though far from refusing the ethical dimension of Sartre's argument, shows that these matters are much more complex than Sartre conceived them. As Barthes says, *écriture* is always "an ambiguous reality: on the one hand, it unquestionably arises from a confrontation of the writer with the society of his time; on the other hand, from this social finality, it refers the writer back, by a sort of tragic reversal, to the sources, that is to say, the instruments of creation."

I have done little more than describe some leading themes of *Writing Degree Zero*. But because of the danger that Barthes' argument will itself be simplified, readers should be warned against being misled by the book's title. That title suggests a rather single-minded manifesto, advocating a stern retrenchment of literature into a desiccated, ascetic noncommunicativeness. This suggestion is likely to be reinforced for those readers aware that Barthes first became well known in France when he emerged as Robbe-Grillet's most eloquent spokesman — notably in three essays, "Le monde-objet" (1953), "Littérature objective" (1954), and "Littérature littérale" (1955), all included in *Essais Critiques* — in which he championed the ingenious and strategic reduction of literary means (i.e. of *style* as Barthes here uses the word) achieved by Robbe-Grillet by de-anthropo-morphizing, eliminating metaphor, etc. But it would be a mistake to read *Writing Degree Zero* merely or even mainly as a polemic preparing the way for the advent of the "solution" of Robbe-Grillet. Actually the notion of zero-degree, neutral, colorless writing — first discussed by Sartre, who called it *l'écriture blanche,* in his famous review of Camus' *L'Etranger*—enters Barthes' argument only briefly: in the introduction (pp. 4–5), as the "last episode of a Passion of writing, which recounts stage by stage the disintegration of bourgeois consciousness," and again at the end (pp. 76–78) as *one* solution to the disintegration of literary language.

But this horizon of literature's final solution is only a boundary-concept, generated by this argument. It is the logical extension of the type of rhetoric Barthes uses. But it is the ground rules of that rhetoric which should be of much more interest and importance to the reader—and have been to Barthes himself, judging from the minor role that the notion of zero-degree writing has played in his subsequent literary studies. What is essential to Barthes' position is not its apocalyptic terminus, but the diagnosis of the over-all situation of literature he makes. Barthes views that peculiarly modern phenomenon of "the multiplication of modes of writing" as an inevitable development. As literature abolishes "more and more its condition as a bourgeois myth," *écriture* pushes aside language and style, absorbing "the whole identity of a literary work." Barthes affirms—and here his thinking strongly reflects the influence of Blanchot—the way literature verges on becoming a total experience, one which brooks no limits, and cannot be permanently stabilized or held in check by any particular strategy of writing, the adoption of zero-degree writing including. As modern literature is the history of alienated "writing" or personal utterance, literature aims inexorably at its own self-transcendence—at the abolition of literature. But Barthes' point would seem to be that no amount of moral exhortation or conceptual unraveling is going to alter drastically this tense, paradoxical state of affairs. "In spite of the efforts made in our time, it has proved impossible successfully to liquidate literature entirely."

This would seem to leave the heaviest burden on the critic, who mediates amid competing chaos—a task Barthes has heroically exemplified in his own ambitious body of work. Thus, in *Writing Degree Zero*, Barthes presupposes both the effort of writers like Valéry, Joyce, Stein, Beckett, and Burroughs to abolish literature and the effort of other writers to confine literature to ethical communication (the notion of "engaged" writing). It is in this agonized suspension between the contradictory goals entertained by literature, I should argue, that the discourse of the responsible critic situates itself—without yielding to an easy dismissal of either position.

Of course, these efforts to liquidate literature have left their trace, which explains the tone, both hectic and detached, with which Barthes approaches his topic. At times, one could describe Barthes' stance in this book as almost an anthropological one, to the extent that he implies that all thinking both about and within literature operates by means of myths. Thus he speaks of the novel as a "mythological object," and of the "rituals" of literature.

The other prominent gesture by which he distances himself from his volatile subject is through constant recourse to a historical perspective. (This is more marked in Part Two of *Writing Degree Zero*, which connects with certain arguments in the latter part of Sartre's book on the historical situation of the contemporary writer, and on writing as a social institution.) But while Barthes shares with Sartre a familiar terminology, adapted from the Hegelian metahistorical scheme of consciousness, *Writing Degree Zero* lacks the detailed, concrete feeling for historical process in evidence in Sartre's book (particularly in the final chapter, "The Situation of the

Writer in 1947"). The history Barthes continually in-
vokes always wears a capital H. This is perhaps the most
serious limit to the argument of *Writing Degree Zero:*
that, while insisting on a historical perspective, Barthes
employs such a generalized, thin notion of history.
Barthes is not so much referring to a real state of affairs
as he is using a metaphor, which allows him to describe
literature as a process rather than as a static entity. The
particular value of history as an organizing myth is that
it provides Barthes with a decisive moment, up to which
the situation he describes leads and from which it pro-
ceeds — a paradigmatic "fall" of literature, which took
place around 1850 and is best incarnated in the consciousness of Flaubert.

Most readers will probably find Part Two of *Writing
Degree Zero* easier going than Part One, because even
Barthes' pseudohistorical concreteness makes the argument somewhat less abstract, and more openly polemical.
(Among the highly effective polemical passages is the
attack on Socialist Realism in the section "Writing and
Revolution.") But it's in Part One that the essentials of
Barthes' view are laid out. Also, Part One suggests more
of Barthes' later thinking, in particular his interest in
consciousness conceived as an arena of classificatory
schemes and systems. The maneuvers of consciousness,
bracketed here by the rather simple notions of "myth"
and "history," are elaborated in Barthes' later books in
the light of Bachelardian phenomenology (*Michelet*)
and Freudian psychology (*Sur Racine*), and, more recently, by approaches which are both ahistorical and
apsychological: contemporary linguistics and the "structuralist" techniques of decoding and classification developed by Lévi-Strauss. The great advantage Barthes
has gained from his new perspective is that anything can

be subjected to the ahistorical, apsychological methods of structuralist analysis. A text does not mean only a literary text, as language is not the only "system of meaning." Thus, in recent years, Barthes has increasingly turned his attention to extra-linguistic languages.*

Barthes' vision of what thinking really is—an insatiable project, endlessly producing and consuming "systems," metaphor-haunted classifications of an ultimately opaque reality—receives only a very elementary exposure in *Writing Degree Zero*. In the present book, he appears at least as much the uncritical accomplice of myths as he is their classifier. Deploying some familiar creative fictions of contemporary intellectual life, such as the Hegelian "history of consciousness," the existentialist "freedom," the Marxist "bourgeois society," etc., Barthes proposes one new myth—that of *écriture*—for the purpose of analyzing a myth, that of "literature." Of course, "myth" doesn't mean that a concept (or argument or narrative) is false. Myths are not descriptions but rather models for description (or thinking)—according to the formula of Lévi-Strauss logical techniques for resolving basic antinomies in thought and social existence. And the converse is also true: all explanatory models for fundamental states of affairs, whether sophisticated or primitive, are myths. From this structuralist point of view, one can't object to *Writing Degree Zero* simply because its leading concepts are intellectual myths or fictions.

* Cf. the essays on Garbo's face, on wine, on detergents, on astrology, on costume, etc., in *Mythologies;* the studies, "La message photographique" in *Communications* No. 1 (1961) and "Rhétorique de l'image" in *Communications* No. 4 (1964), which deal mainly with advertising texts, to the recent big book, *Système de la Mode* (1967), which examines the classificatory systems implicit in women's clothing as reflected in the language used in fashion magazines.

What matters is that Barthes' myths about literature are extremely talented, even masterful, and do satisfy the need for intellectual cohesion (comparable to the way myths in the more ordinary sense, according to Lévi-Strauss, produce social cohesion).

After all, it isn't Barthes who made "literature" into a myth. He found it in that condition, along with all the other arts in our time. Someday perhaps a demystification of the myth of "art" (as an absolute activity) will be possible and will take place, but it seems far from that moment now. At this stage, only new myths can subdue — even for the brief time to permit contemplation — the old myths which move convulsively about us. Measured on this scale of need, the myths about literature proposed in *Writing Degree Zero* seem to me sturdy, subtle, and highly serviceable. They acknowledge basic antinomies that even the most gifted minds addressing the same subject, such as Sartre, have glossed over. And to anyone seriously caught up in the lacerating dialectics imposed by the stand of advanced art and consciousness in our time, the myths/models deployed by Barthes can also be recommended for their healing, therapeutic value.

SUSAN SONTAG

INTRODUCTION

Hébert, the revolutionary, never began a number of his news-sheet *Le Père Duchêne* without introducing a sprinkling of obscenities. These improprieties had no real meaning, but they had significance. In what way? In that they expressed a whole revolutionary situation. Now here is an example of a mode of writing* whose function is no longer only communication or expression, but the imposition of something beyond language, which is both History and the stand we take in it.

It is impossible to write without labelling oneself: as with *Le Père Duchêne*, so equally with Literature. It too must signify something other than its content and its individual form, something which defines its

* *Ecriture*, which in French normally means only 'handwriting' or 'the art of writing', is now more and more frequently used as a substantive corresponding to all senses of the verb *écrire*, generally to mean the style, the fact of composing a work, or the actions which properly belong to a writer. It is used here in a strictly technical sense to denote a new concept, and is translated as 'writing', 'mode of writing'. This concept is discussed further in relation to that of 'idiolect' in *Elements of Semiology* (I.1.6 and I.1.7), as is that of 'zero degree'.

limits and imposes it as Literature. Whence a set of signs unrelated to the ideas, the language or the style, and setting out to give definition, within the body of every possible mode of expression, to the utter separateness of a ritual language. This hieratic quality of written Signs establishes Literature as an institution and clearly tends to place it above History, for no limits can be set without some idea of permanence. Now it is when History is denied that it is most unmistakably at work; it is therefore possible to trace a history of literary expression which is neither that of a particular language, nor that of the various styles, but simply that of the Signs of Literature, and we can expect that this purely formal history may manifest, in its far from obscure way, a link with the deeper levels of History.

We are naturally concerned with a link the form of which may well vary with History itself; there is no need to invoke direct determinism in order to feel that History underlies the fortunes of modes of writing: this kind of functional front, which sweeps along events, situations and ideas in the current of historical time, does not so much produce effects as set limits to choice. History, then, confronts the writer with a necessary option between several moral attitudes connected with language; it forces him to signify Literature in terms of possibilities outside his control. We shall see, for example, that the ideological unity of the bourgeoisie gave rise to a single mode of writing, and that in the bourgeois periods (classical and romantic), literary form could not be divided because consciousness was not; whereas, as soon as the writer ceased to be a witness to the universal, to become the incarnation of a tragic awareness (around 1850), his first gesture was to choose the commitment of his form, either by adopting or rejecting the writing of his past. Classical writing therefore disintegrated, and the whole of Literature, from Flaubert to the present day, became the problematics of language.

This was precisely the time when Literature (the word having come into being shortly before) was finally established as an object. Classical art could have no sense of being a language, for it *was* language, in other words it was transparent, it flowed and left no deposit, it brought ideally together a universal Spirit and a decorative sign without substance or responsibility; it was a language 'closed' by social and not natural bounds. It is a well-known fact that towards the end of the eighteenth century this transparency becomes clouded; literary form develops a second-order power independent of its economy and euphemistic charm; it fascinates the reader, it strikes him as exotic, it enthralls him, it acquires a weight. Literature is no longer felt as a socially privileged mode of transaction, but as a language having body and hidden depths, existing both as dream and menace.

This is important: literary form may henceforth elicit those existential feelings lying at the heart of any object: a sense of strangeness or familiarity, disgust or indulgence, utility or murder. For a century now, every mode of writing has thus been an exercise in reconciliation with, or aversion from, that objectified Form inevitably met by the writer on his way, and which he must scrutinize, challenge and accept with all its consequences, since he cannot ever destroy it without destroying himself as a writer. Form hovers before his gaze like an object; whatever he does, it is a scandal: if it stands resplendent, it appears outmoded; if it is a law unto itself, it is asocial; in so far as it is particular in relation to time or mankind, it cannot but mean solitude.

The whole nineteenth century witnessed the progress of this dramatic phenomenon of concretion. In Chateaubriand it is still only a trace, a light pressure of linguistic euphoria, a kind of narcissism in which the manner of writing is scarcely separable from its instrumental function and merely mirrors itself. Flaubert – to take only the typical stages of this process – finally established Literature as an object, through promoting literary labour to the status of a value; form became the end-product of craftsmanship, like a piece of pottery or a jewel (one must understand that craftsmanship was here made manifest, that is, it was for the first time imposed on the reader as a spectacle). Mallarmé's work, finally, was the

4

crowning achievement of this creation of Literature as Object, and this by the ultimate of all objectifying acts: murder. For we know that the whole effort of Mallarmé was exerted towards the destruction of language, with Literature reduced, so to speak, to being its carcass.

From an initial non-existence in which thought, by a happy miracle, seemed to stand out against the backcloth of words, writing thus passed through all the stages of a progressive solidification; it was first the object of a gaze, then of creative action, finally of murder, and has reached in our time a last metamorphosis, absence: in those neutral modes of writing, called here 'the zero degree of writing', we can easily discern a negative momentum, and an inability to maintain it within time's flow, as if Literature, having tended for a hundred years now to transmute its surface into a form with no antecedents, could no longer find purity anywhere but in the absence of all signs, finally proposing the realization of this Orphean dream: a writer without Literature. Colourless writing like Camus's, Blanchot's or Cayrol's, for example, or conversational writing like Queneau's, represents the last episode of a Passion of writing, which recounts stage by stage the disintegration of bourgeois consciousness.

What we hope to do here is to sketch this connection; to affirm the existence of a formal reality independent of language and style; to try to show that this third dimension of Form equally, and not without an additional tragic implication, binds the writer to his society; finally to convey the fact that there is no Literature without an Ethic of language. The limited length of this essay (a few pages of which appeared in 1947 and 1950 in *Combat*) is sufficient indication that what is offered here is no more than an Introduction to what a History of Writing might be.

Part One

WHAT IS WRITING?

We know that a language is a corpus of pre-scriptions and habits common to all the writers of a period. Which means that a language is a kind of natural ambience wholly pervading the writer's expression, yet without endowing it with form or content: it is, as it were, an abstract circle of truths, outside of which alone the solid residue of an individual *logos* begins to settle. It enfolds the whole of literary creation much as the earth, the sky and the line where they meet outline a familiar habitat for mankind. It is not so much a stock of materials as a horizon, which implies both a boundary and a perspective; in short, it is the comforting area of an ordered space. The writer literally takes nothing from it; a language is for him rather a frontier, to overstep which alone might lead to the linguistically supernatural; it is a field of action, the definition of, and hope for, a possibility. It is not the locus of a social commitment, but merely a reflex response involving no choice, the undivided property of men, not of writers; it remains outside the ritual of Letters; it is a social object by definition, not by option. No one can without formalities pretend to insert his freedom as a writer into the resistant medium of language because, behind the latter, the whole of History stands unified and complete in the manner of a Natural Order. Hence, for the writer, a language is nothing but a human horizon which provides a distant setting of *familiarity*, the value of which, incidentally, is entirely negative: to say that Camus and Queneau speak the same language is merely to presume, by a differential operation, all languages, archaic and futuristic, that they do not use. Suspended between forms either disused or as yet unknown, the writer's language is not so much a fund to be drawn on as an extreme limit; it is the geometrical *locus* of all that he could not say without, like Orpheus looking back, losing the stable meaning of his enterprise and his essential gesture as a social being.

A language is therefore on the hither side of Literature. Style is almost beyond it: imagery, delivery, vocabulary spring from the body and the past of the writer and gradually become the very reflexes of his art. Thus under the name of style a self-sufficient language is evolved which has its roots only in the depths of the author's personal and secret mythology, that subnature of expression where the first coition of words and things takes place, where once and for all the great verbal themes of his existence come to be installed. Whatever its sophistication, style has always something crude about it: it is a form with no clear destination, the product of a thrust, not an intention, and, as it were, a vertical and lonely dimension of thought. Its frame of reference is biological or biographical, not historical: it is the writer's 'thing', his glory and his prison, it is his solitude. Indifferent to society and transparent to it, a closed personal process, it is in no way the product of a choice or of a reflection on Literature. It is the private portion of the ritual, it rises up from the writer's myth-laden depths and unfolds beyond his area of control. It is the decorative voice of hidden, secret flesh; it works as does Necessity, as if, in this kind of floral growth, style were no more than the outcome of a blind and stubborn metamorphosis starting from a sub-language elaborated where flesh and external reality come together. Style is properly speaking a germinative phenomenon, the transmutation of a Humour. Hence stylistic overtones are distributed in depth; whereas speech has a horizontal structure, its secrets are on a level with the words in which they are couched, and what it conceals is revealed by the very duration of its flow. In speech, everything is held forth, meant for immediate consumption, and words, silences and their common mobility are launched towards a meaning superseded: it is a transfer leaving no trace and brooking no delay. Style, on the other hand, has only a vertical dimension, it plunges into the closed recollection of the person and achieves its opacity from a certain experience of matter; style is never anything but metaphor, that is, equivalence of the author's literary intention and carnal structure (it must be remembered that structure is the residual deposit of duration). So that style is always a secret; but the occult aspect of its implications does not arise from the mobile and ever-provisional nature of language; its secret is recollection locked within the body of the writer. The allusive virtue of style is not a matter of speed, as in speech, where what is unsaid nevertheless remains as an interim of language, but a matter of density, for what stands firmly and deeply beneath style, brought together harshly or tenderly in its figures of speech, are fragments of a reality entirely alien to language. The miracle of this transmutation makes style a kind of supra-literary operation which carries man to the threshold of power and magic. By reason of its biological origin, style resides outside art, that is, outside the pact which binds the writer to society. Authors may therefore be imagined who prefer the security of art to the loneliness of style. The very type of an author without a style is Gide, whose craftsmanlike approach exploits the pleasure the moderns derive from a certain classical ethos, just as Saint-Saëns has composed in Bach's idiom, or Poulenc in Schubert's. In contrast, modern poetry – such as Hugo's, Rimbaud's or Char's – is saturated with style and is *art* only by virtue of an intention to be Poetry. It is the Authority of style, that is, the entirely free relationship between language and its fleshly double, which places the writer above History as the freshness of Innocence.

A language is therefore a horizon, and style a vertical dimension, which together map out for the writer a Nature, since he does not choose either. The language functions negatively, as the initial limit of the possible, style is a Necessity which binds the writer's humour to his form of expression. In the former, he finds a familiar History, in the latter, a familiar personal past. In both cases he deals with a Nature, that is, a familiar repertory of gestures, a gestuary, as it were, in which the energy expended is purely operative, serving here to enumerate, there to transform, but never to appraise or signify a choice.

Now every Form is also a Value, which is why there is room, between a language and a style, for another formal reality: writing. Within any literary form, there is a general choice of tone, of ethos, if you like, and this is precisely where the writer shows himself clearly as an individual because this is where he commits himself. A language and a style are data prior to all problematics of language, they are the natural product of Time and of the person as a biological entity; but the formal identity of the writer is truly established only outside the permanence of grammatical norms and stylistic constants, where the written continuum, first collected and enclosed within a perfectly innocent linguistic nature, at last becomes a total sign, the choice of a human attitude, the affirmation of a certain Good. It thus commits the writer to manifest and communicate a state of happiness or malaise, and links the form of his utterance, which is at once normal and singular, to the vast History of the Others. A language and a style are blind forces; a mode of writing is an act of historical solidarity. A language and a style are objects; a mode of writing is a function: it is the relationship between creation and society, the literary language transformed by its social finality, form considered as a human intention and thus linked to the great crises of History. Mérimée and Fénelon, for instance, are separated by linguistic phenomena and contingent features of style; yet they make use of a language charged with the same intentionality, their ideas of form and content share a common framework, they accept the same type of conventions, the same technical reflexes work through both of them. Although separated by a century and a half, they use exactly the same instrument in the same way: an instrument perhaps a little changed in outward appearance, but not at all in the place and manner of its employment. In short, they have the same mode of writing. In contrast, writers who are almost contemporaries, Mérimée and Lautréamont, Mallarmé and Céline, Gide and Queneau, Claudel and Camus, who have shared or who share our language at the same stage of its historical development use utterly different modes of writing. Everything separates them: tone, delivery, purpose, ethos, and naturalness of expression: the conclusion is that to live at the same time and share the same language is a small matter compared with modes of writing so dissimilar and so sharply defined by their very dissimilarity.

These modes of writing, though different, are comparable, because they owe their existence to one identical process, namely the writer's consideration of the social use which he has chosen for his form, and his commitment to this choice. Placed at the centre of the problematics of literature, which cannot exist prior to it, writing is thus essentially the morality of form, the choice of that social area within which the writer elects to situate the Nature of his language. But this social area is by no means that of an actual consumption. It is not a question for the writer of choosing the social group for which he is to write: well he knows that, save for the possibility of a Revolution, it can only be for the self same society. His choice is a matter of conscience, not of efficacy. His writing is a way of conceiving Literature, not of extending its limits. Or better still: it is because the writer cannot modify in any way the objective data which govern the consumption of literature (these purely historical data are beyond his control even if

15

he is aware of them), that <u>he voluntarily places the need for a free language at the sources of this language</u> and not in its eventual consumption. So that writing is an ambiguous reality : on the one hand, it unquestionably arises from a confrontation of the writer with the society of his time; on the other hand, from this social finality, it refers the writer back, by a sort of tragic reversal, to the sources, that is to say, the instruments of creation. Failing the power to supply him with a freely consumed language, History suggests to him the demand for one freely produced.

Thus the choice of, and afterwards the responsibility for, a mode of writing point to the presence of Freedom, but this Freedom has not the same limits at different moments of History. It is not granted to the writer to choose his mode of writing from a kind of non-temporal store of literary forms. It is under the pressure of History and Tradition that the possible modes of writing for a given writer are established; there is a History of Writing. But this History is dual : at the very moment when general History proposes – or imposes – new problematics of the literary language, writing still remains full of the recollection of previous usage, for language is never innocent : words have a second-order memory which mysteriously persists in the midst of new meanings. Writing is precisely this compromise between freedom and remembrance, it is this freedom which remembers and is free only in the gesture of choice, but is no

16

[Handwritten marginal notes, left margin, top to bottom:] "Or" there is "no" audience – or none really, that matters. as soon the writer supposes one, a writer "one" he is trying to change objectin at the consumption and of language – he is in a strange yet very real sense, no longer a writer when he has this – he is a revolutionary or a propagandist or a shill for one idea or another – language is no longer an object ; but has reverted to the speech the writer was "born with" longer so within duration. True, I can today select such and such mode of writing, and in so doing assert my freedom, aspire to the freshness of novelty or to a tradition; but it is impossible to develop it within duration without gradually becoming a prisoner of someone else's words and even of my own. A stubborn after-image, which comes from all the previous modes of writing and even from the past of my own, drowns the sound of my present words. Any written trace precipitates, as inside a chemical at first transparent, innocent and neutral, mere duration gradually reveals in suspension a whole past of increasing density, like a cryptogram.

Writing as Freedom is therefore a mere moment. But this moment is one of the most explicit in History, since History is always and above all a choice and the limits of this choice. It is because writing derives from a meaningful gesture of the writer that it reaches the deeper layers of History, much more palpably than does any other cross-section of literature. The unity of classical writing, which remained uniform for centuries, the plurality of its modes in modern times, increased in the last hundred years until it came near to questioning the very fact of literature, this kind of disintegration of French writing does indeed correspond to a great crisis in general History, which is noticeable in literary History proper, only much more confusedly. What separates the 'thought' of a Balzac from that of a Flaubert is a variation within the same school; what contrasts their modes of writing is an essential break, at the precise moment when a new economic structure is joined on to an older one, thereby bringing about decisive changes in mentality and consciousness.

POLITICAL MODES OF
WRITING

All modes of writing have in common the fact of being 'closed' and thus different from spoken language. Writing is in no way an instrument for communication, it is not an open route through which there passes only the intention to speak. A whole disorder flows through speech and gives it this self-devouring momentum which keeps it in a perpetually suspended state. Conversely, writing is a hardened language which is self-contained and is in no way meant to deliver to its own duration a mobile series of approximations. It is on the contrary meant to impose, thanks to the shadow cast by its system of signs, the image of a speech which had a structure even before it came into existence. What makes writing the opposite of speech is that the former always *appears* symbolical, introverted, ostensibly turned towards an occult side of language, whereas the second is nothing but a flow of empty signs, the movement of which alone is significant. The whole of speech is epitomized in this expendability of words, in this froth ceaselessly swept onwards, and speech is found only where language self-evidently functions like a devouring process which swallows only the moving crest of the words. Writing, on the contrary, is always rooted in something beyond language, it develops like a seed, not like a line, it manifests an essence and holds the threat of a secret, it is an anti-communication, it is intimidating. All writing will therefore contain the ambiguity of an object which is both language and coercion: there exists fundamentally in writing a 'circumstance' foreign to language, there is, as it were, the weight of a gaze conveying an intention which is no longer linguistic. This gaze may well express a passion of language, as in literary modes of writing; it may also express the threat of retribution, as in political ones: writing is then meant to unite at a single stroke the reality of the acts and the ideality of the ends. This is why power, or the shadow cast by power, always ends in creating an axiological writing, in which the distance which usually separates fact from value disappears within the very space of the word, which is given at once as description and as judgment. The word becomes an alibi, that is, an elsewhere and a justification. This, which is true of the literary modes of writing, in which the unity of the signs is ceaselessly fascinated by zones of infra- or ultra-language, is even truer of the political ones, in which the alibi stemming from language is at the same time intimidation and glorification: for it is power or conflict which produce the purest types of writing.

We shall see later that classical writing was a ceremonial which manifested the implantation of the writer into a particular political society, and that to speak like Vaugelas meant in the first place to be connected with the exercise of power. The Revolution did not modify the norms of this writing, since its force of thinkers remained, all things considered, the same, having merely passed from intellectual to political power; but the exceptional conditions of the struggle nevertheless brought about, within the great Form of classicism, a revolutionary mode of writing proper, defined not by its structure (which was more conventional than ever) but by its closed character and by its counterpart, since the use of language was then linked, as never before in history, to the Blood which had been shed. The Revolutionaries had no reason to wish to alter classical writing; they were in no way aware of questioning the nature of man, still less his language, and an 'instrument' they had inherited from Voltaire, Rousseau or Vauvenargues could not appear to them as compromised. It was the singularity of the historical circumstances which produced the identity of the revolutionary mode of writing. Baudelaire spoke somewhere of the 'grandiloquent truth of gestures on life's great occasions'. The Revolution was in the highest degree one of those great occasions when truth, through the bloodshed that it costs, becomes so weighty that its expression demands the very forms of theatrical amplification.

Revolutionary writing was the one and only grand gesture commensurate with the daily presence of the guillotine. What today appears turgid was then no more than life-size. This writing, which bears all the signs of inflation, was an exact writing: never was language more incredible, yet never was it less spurious. This grandiloquence was not only form modelled on drama; it was also the awareness of it. Without this extravagant pose, typical of all the great revolutionaries, which enabled Guadet, the Girondin, when arrested at Saint-Emilion, to declare without looking ridiculous, since he was about to die: 'Yes, I am Guadet. Executioner, do your duty. Go take my head to the tyrants of my country. It has always turned them pale; once severed, it will turn them paler still', the Revolution could not have been this mythical event which made History fruitful, along with all future ideas on revolution. Revolutionary writing was so to speak the entelechy of the revolutionary legend: it struck fear into men's hearts and imposed upon them a citizen's sacrament of Bloodshed.

Marxist writing is of a different order. Here the closed character of the form does not derive from rhetorical amplification or from grandiloquence in delivery, but from a lexicon as specialized and as functional as a technical vocabulary; even metaphors

22

are here severely codified. French revolutionary writing always proclaimed a right founded on bloodshed or moral justification, whereas from the very start Marxist writing is presented as the language of knowledge. Here, writing is univocal, because it is meant to maintain the cohesion of a Nature; it is the lexical identity of this writing which allows it to impose a stability in its explanations and a permanence in its method; it is only in the light of its whole linguistic system that Marxism is perceived in all its political implications. Marxist writing is as much given to understatement as revolutionary writing is to grandiloquence, since each word is no longer anything but a narrow reference to the set of principles which tacitly underlie it. For instance, the word 'imply', frequently encountered in Marxist writing, does not there have its neutral dictionary meaning; it always refers to a precise historical process, and is like an algebraical sign representing a whole bracketed set of previous postulates.

Being linked to action, Marxist writing has rapidly become, in fact, a language expressing value-judgments. This character, already visible in Marx, whose writing however remains in general explanatory, has come to pervade writing completely in the era of triumphant Stalinism. Certain outwardly similar notions, for which a neutral vocabulary would not seek a dual designation, are evaluatively parted from each other, so that each element gravitates towards a different noun: for instance, 'cosmopolitanism' is the negative of 'internationalism' (already in Marx). In the Stalinist world, in which *definition*, that is to say the separation between Good and Evil, becomes the sole content of all language, there are no more words without values attached to them, so that finally the function of writing is to cut out one stage of a process: there is no more lapse of time between naming and judging, and the closed character of language is perfected, since in the last analysis it is a value which is given as explanation of another value. For instance, it may be alleged that such and such a criminal has engaged in activities harmful to the interests of the state; which boils down to saying that a criminal is someone who commits a crime. We see that this is in fact a tautology, a device constantly used in Stalinist writing. For the latter no longer aims at founding a Marxist version of the facts, or a revolutionary rationale of actions, but at presenting reality in a prejudged form, thus imposing a reading which involves immediate condemnation: the objective content of the word 'deviationist' puts it into a penological category. If two deviationists band together, they become 'fractionists', which does not involve an objectively different crime, but an increase in the sentence imposed. One can enumerate a properly Marxist writing (that of Marx and Lenin) and a writing of triumphant Stalinism; there certainly is as well a Trotskyist writing and a tactical writing, for instance that of the French Communist party with its substitution of 'people', then of 'plain folk', for 'working class', and the wilful ambiguity of terms like 'democracy', 'freedom', 'peace', etc.

There is no doubt at all that each regime has its own writing, no history of which has yet been written. Since writing is the spectacular commitment of language, it contains at one and the same time, thanks to a valuable ambiguity, the reality and the appearance of power, what it is, and what it would like to be thought to be: a history of political modes of writing would therefore be the best of social phenomenologies. For instance, the French Restoration evolved a class writing by means of which repression was immediately given as a condemnation spontaneously arising from classical 'Nature': workers claiming rights were always 'troublemakers', strike-breakers were 'good workmen', and the subservience of judges became, in this language, the 'paternal vigilance of magistrates' (it is thanks to a similar procedure that Gaullism today calls Communists 'separatists'). We see that here the function of writing is to maintain a clear conscience and that its mission is fraudulently to identify the original fact with its remotest subsequent transformation by bolstering up the justification of actions with the additional guarantee of its own reality. This fact about writing is, by the way, typical of all authoritarian regimes; it is what might be called police-state writing: we know, for example, that the content of the word 'Order' always indicates repression.

The spreading influence of political and social facts into the literary field of consciousness has produced a new type of scriptor, halfway between the party member and the writer, deriving from the former an ideal image of committed man, and from the latter the notion that a written work is an act. Thus while the intellectual supersedes the writer, there appears in periodicals and in essays a militant mode of writing entirely freed from stylistic considerations, and which is, so to speak, a professional language signifying 'presence'. In this mode of writing, nuances abound. Nobody will deny that there is such a thing, for instance, as a writing typical of *Esprit* or of *Les Temps Modernes*.* What these intellectual modes of writing have in common, is that in them language, instead of being a privileged area, tends to become the sufficient sign of commitment. To come to adopt a closed sphere of language under the pressure of all those who do not speak it, is to proclaim one's act of choosing, if not necessarily one's agreement with that choice. Writing here resembles the signature one

* *Esprit* and *Les Temps Modernes* are two prominent monthlies, the first Left-wing Catholic and the second directed by J.-P. Sartre.

affixes at the foot of a collective proclamation one has not written oneself. So that to adopt a mode of writing – or, even better, to make it one's own – means to save oneself all the preliminaries of a choice, and to make it quite clear that one takes for granted the reasons for such a choice. Any intellectual writing is therefore the first of the 'leaps of the intellect'. Whereas an ideally free language never could function as a sign of my own person and would give no information whatsoever about my history and my freedom, the writing to which I entrust myself already exists entirely as an institution; it reveals my past and my choice, it gives me a history, it blazons forth my situation, it commits me without my having to declare the fact. Form thus becomes more than ever an autonomous object, meant to signify a property which is collective and protected, and this object is a trouble-saving device: it functions as an economy signal whereby the scriptor constantly imposes his conversion without ever revealing how it came about.

This duplicity of today's intellectual modes of writing is emphasized by the fact that in spite of the efforts made in our time, it has proved impossible successfully to liquidate Literature entirely: it still constitutes a verbal horizon commanding respect. The intellectual is still only an incompletely transformed writer, and unless he scuttles himself and becomes for ever a militant who no longer writes (some

27

have done so, and are therefore forgotten), he cannot but come back to the fascination of former modes of writing, transmitted through Literature as an instrument intact but obsolete. These intellectual modes of writing are therefore unstable, they remain literary to the extent that they are powerless, and are political only through their obsession with commitment. In short, we are still dealing with ethical modes of writing, in which the conscience of the scriptor (one no longer ventures to call him a writer) finds the comforting image of collective salvation.

But just as, in the present state of History, any political mode of writing can only uphold a police world, so any intellectual mode of writing can only give rise to a para-literature, which no longer dares to speak its name. Both are therefore in a complete blind alley, they can lead only to complicity or impotence, which means, in either case, to alienation.

WRITING AND THE NOVEL

The Novel and History have been closely related in the very century which witnessed their greatest development. Their link in depth, that which should allow us to understand at once Balzac and Michelet, is that in both we find the construction of an autarkic world which elaborates its own dimensions and limits, and organizes within these its own Time, its own Space, its population, its own set of objects and its myths.

This sphericity of the great works of the nineteenth century found its expression in those long recitatives, the Novel and History, which are, as it were, plane projections of a curved and organic world of which the serial story which came into being at that precise moment, presents, through its involved complications, a degraded image. And yet narration is not necessarily a law of the form. A whole period could conceive novels in letters, for instance; and another can evolve a practice of History by means of analyses. Therefore Narration, as a form common to both the Novel and to History, does remain, in general, the choice or the expression of an historical moment.

Obsolete in spoken French, the preterite, which is the cornerstone of Narration, always signifies the presence of Art; it is a part of a ritual of Letters. Its function is no longer that of a tense. The part it plays is to reduce reality to a point of time, and to abstract, from the depth of a multiplicity of experiences, a pure verbal act, freed from the existential roots of knowledge, and directed towards a logical link with other acts, other processes, a general movement of the world: it aims at maintaining a hierarchy in the realm of facts. Through the preterite, the verb implicitly belongs with a causal chain, it partakes of a set of related and orientated actions, it functions as the algebraic sign of an intention. Allowing as it does an ambiguity between temporality and causality, it calls for a sequence of events, that is, for an intelligible Narrative. This is why it is the ideal instrument for every construction of a world; it is the unreal time of cosmogonies, myths, History and Novels. It presupposes a world which is constructed, elaborated, self-sufficient, reduced to significant lines, and not one which has been sent sprawling before us, for us to take or leave. Behind the preterite there always lurks a demiurge, a God or a reciter. The world is not unexplained since it is told like a story; each one of its accidents is but a circumstance, and the preterite is precisely this operative sign whereby the narrator reduces the exploded reality to a slim and pure logos, without density, without volume, without spread, and whose sole function is to unite as rapidly as possible a cause and an end. When the historian states that the duc de Guise died on December 23rd, 1588, or when the novelist relates that the Marchioness went out at five o'clock,* such actions emerge from a past without substance; purged of the uncertainty of existence, they have the stability and outline of an algebra, they are a recollection, but a useful recollection, the interest of which far surpasses its duration.

So that finally the preterite is the expression of an order, and consequently of a euphoria. Thanks to it, reality is neither mysterious nor absurd; it is clear, almost familiar, repeatedly gathered up and contained in the hand of a creator; it is subjected to the ingenious pressure of his freedom. For all the great storytellers of the nineteenth century, the world may be full of pathos but it is not derelict, since it is a grouping of coherent relations, since there is no overlapping between the written facts, since he who tells the story has the power to do away with the opacity and the solitude of the existences which made it up, since he can in all sentences bear witness to a communication and a hierarchy of actions and since, to tell the truth, these very actions can be reduced to mere signs.

---

* The sentence which for Valéry epitomized the conventions of the novel.

The narrative past is therefore a part of a security system for Belles-Lettres. Being the image of an order, it is one of those numerous formal pacts made between the writer and society for the justification of the former and the serenity of the latter. The preterite *signifies* a creation: that is, it proclaims and imposes it. Even from the depth of the most sombre realism, it has a reassuring effect because, thanks to it, the verb expresses a closed, well-defined, substantival act, the Novel has a name, it escapes the terror of an expression without laws: reality becomes slighter and more familiar, it fits within a style, it does not outrun language. Literature remains the currency in use in a society apprised, by the very form of words, of the meaning of what it consumes. On the contrary, when the Narrative is rejected in favour of other literary genres, or when, within the narration, the preterite is replaced by less ornamental forms, fresher, more full-blooded and nearer to speech (the present tense or the present perfect), Literature becomes the receptacle of existence in all its density and no longer of its meaning alone. The acts it recounts are still separated from History, but no longer from people.

We now understand what is profitable and what is intolerable in the preterite as used in the Novel: it is a lie made manifest, it delineates an area of plausibility which reveals the possible in the very act of unmasking it as false. The teleology common to the

Novel and to narrated History is the alienation of the facts: the preterite is the very act by which society affirms its possession of its past and its possibility. It creates a content credible, yet flaunted as an illusion; it is the ultimate term of a formal dialectics which clothes an unreal fact in the garb first of truth then of a lie denounced as such. This has to be related to a certain mythology of the universal typifying the bourgeois society of which the Novel is a characteristic product; it involves giving to the imaginary the formal guarantee of the real, but while preserving in the sign the ambiguity of a double object, at once believable and false. This operation occurs constantly in the whole of Western art, in which the false is equal to the true, not through any agnosticism or poetic duplicity, but because the true is supposed to contain a germ of the universal, or to put it differently, an essence capable of fecundating by mere reproduction, several orders of things among which some differ by their remoteness and some by their fictitious character.

It is thanks to an expedient of the same kind that the triumphant bourgeoisie of the last century was able to look upon its values as universal and to carry over to sections of society which were absolutely heterogeneous to it all the Names which were parts of its ethos. This is strictly how myths function, and the Novel – and within the Novel, the preterite – are mythological objects in which there is, superimposed

33

upon an immediate intention, a second-order appeal
to a corpus of dogmas, or better, to a pedagogy, since
what is sought is to impart an essence in the guise of
an artefact. In order to grasp the significance of the
preterite, we have but to compare the Western art of
the novel with a certain Chinese tradition, for instance, in which art lies solely in the perfection with
which reality is imitated. But in this tradition no sign,
absolutely nothing, must allow any distinction to be
drawn between the natural and the artificial objects:
this wooden walnut must not impart to me, along
with the image of a walnut, the intention of conveying to me the art which gave birth to it. Whereas on
the contrary this is what writing does in the novel. Its
task is to put the mask in place and at the same time
to point it out.

This ambiguous function disclosed in the preterite
is found in another fact relating to this type of writing: the third person in the Novel. The reader will
perhaps recall a novel by Agatha Christie in which all
the invention consisted in concealing the murderer
beneath the use of the first person of the narrative.
The reader looked for him behind every 'he' in the
plot: he was all the time hidden under the 'I'. Agatha
Christie knew perfectly well that, in the novel, the 'I'
is usually a spectator, and that it is the 'he' who is the

actor. Why? The 'he' is a typical novelistic convention; like the narrative tense, it signifies and
carries through the action of the novel; if the third
person is absent, the novel is powerless to come into
being, and even wills its own destruction. The 'he' is a
formal manifestation of the myth, and we have just
seen that, in the West at least, there is no art which
does not point to its own mask. The third person, like
the preterite, therefore performs this service for the
art of the novel, and supplies its consumers with the
security born of a credible fabrication which is yet
constantly held up as false.

Less ambiguous, the 'I' is thereby less typical of the
novel: it is therefore at the same time the most obvious solution, when the narration remains on this
side of convention (Proust's work, for instance, pur-
ports to be a mere introduction to Literature), and the
most sophisticated, when the 'I' takes its place beyond convention and attempts to destroy it, by con-
ferring on the narrative the spurious naturalness of
taking the reader into its confidence (such is the guile-
ful air of some stories by Gide). In the same way the
use of the 'he' in a novel involves two opposed
systems of ethics: since it represents an unquestioned
convention, it attracts the most conformist and the
least dissatisfied, as well as those others who have
decided that, finally, this convention is necessary to
the novelty of their work. In any case, it is the sign of
an intelligible pact between society and the author;

35

but it is also, for the latter, the most important means he has of building the world in the way that he chooses. It is therefore more than a literary experiment : it is a human act which connects creation to History or to existence.

In Balzac for instance, the multiplicity of 'he's', this vast network of characters, slight in terms of solid flesh, but consistent by the duration of their acts, reveals the existence of a world of which History is the first datum. The Balzacian 'he' is not the end-product of a development starting from some transformed and generalized 'I'; it is the original and crude element of the novel, the material, not the outcome, the creative activity : there is no Balzacian history prior to the history of each third person in the novels of Balzac. His 'he' is analogous to Caesar's 'he' : the third person here brings about a kind of algebraic state of the action, in which existence plays the smallest possible part, in favour of elements which connect, clarify, or show the tragedy inherent in human relationships. Conversely – or at any rate previously – the function of 'he' in the novel can be that of expressing an existential experience. In many modern novelists the history of the man is identified with the course of the conjugation : starting from an 'I' which is still the form which expresses anonymity most faithfully, man and author little by little win the right to the third person, in proportion as existence becomes fate, and soliloquy becomes a

Novel. Here the appearance of the 'he' is not the starting point of History, it is the end of an effort which has been successful in extracting from a personal world made up of humours and tendencies, a form which is pure, significant, and which therefore vanishes as soon as it is born thanks to the totally conventional and ethereal decor of the third person. This certainly was the course displayed in the first novels of Jean Cayrol whose case can be taken as an exemplar. But whereas in the classics – and we know that where writing is concerned classicism lasts until Flaubert – the withdrawal of the biological person testifies to the establishment of essential man, in novelists such as Cayrol, the invasion of the 'he' is a progressive conquest over the profound darkness of the existential 'I': so true it is that the Novel, identified as it is by its most formal signs, is a gesture of sociability; it establishes Literature as an institution.

Maurice Blanchot has shown, in the case of Kafka, that the elaboration of the impersonal narrative (let us notice, apropos of this term, that the 'third person' is always presented as a negative degree of the person) was an act of fidelity to the essence of language, since the latter naturally tends towards its own destruction. We therefore understand how 'he' is a victory over 'I', inasmuch as it conjures up a state at once more literary and more absent. None the less this victory is ceaselessly threatened: the literary convention of the 'he' is necessary to the belittling of the person, but runs at every moment the risk of encumbering it with an unexpected density. For Literature is like phosphorus: it shines with its maximum brilliance at the moment when it attempts to die. But as, on the other hand, it is an act which necessarily implies a duration – especially in the Novel – there can never be any Novel independently of Belles-Lettres. So that the third person in the Novel is one of the most obsessive signs of this tragic aspect of writing which was born in the last century, when under the weight of History, Literature became dissociated from the society which consumes it. Between the third person as used by Balzac and that used by Flaubert, there is a world of difference (that of 1848): in the former we have a view of History which is harsh, but coherent and certain of its principles, the triumph of an order; in the latter, an art which in order to escape its pangs of conscience either exaggerates conventions or frantically attempts to destroy them. Modernism begins with the search for a Literature which is no longer possible.

Thus we find, in the Novel too, this machinery directed towards both destruction and resurrection, and typical of the whole of modern art. What must be destroyed is duration, that is, the ineffable binding force running through existence: for order, whether it be that of poetic flow or of narrative signs, that of Terror or plausibility, is always a murder in intention. But what reconquers the writer is again duration, for it is impossible to develop a negative within time, without elaborating a positive art, an order which must be destroyed anew. So that the greater modern works linger as long as possible, in a sort of miraculous stasis, on the threshold of Literature, in this anticipatory state in which the breadth of life is given, stretched but not yet destroyed by this crowning phase, an order of signs. For instance, we have the first person in Proust, whose whole work rests on a slow and protracted effort towards Literature. We have Jean Cayrol, whose acquiescence to the Novel comes only as the very last stage of soliloquy, as if the literary act, being supremely ambiguous, could be delivered of a creation consecrated by society, only at the moment when it has at last succeeded in destroying the existential density of a hitherto meaningless duration.

The Novel is a Death; it transforms life into destiny, a memory into a useful act, duration into an orientated and meaningful time. But this transformation can be accomplished only in full view of society. It is society which imposes the Novel, that is, a complex of signs, as a transcendence and as the History of a duration. It is therefore by the obviousness of its intention, grasped in that of the narrative signs, that one can recognize the path which, through all the solemnity of art, binds the writer to society. The preterite and the third person in the Novel are nothing but the fateful gesture with which the writer draws attention to the mask which he is wearing. The whole of Literature can declare *Larvatus prodeo*,* As I walk forward, I point out my mask. Whether we deal with the inhuman experience of the poet, who accepts the most momentous of all breaks, that from the language of society, or with the plausible untruth of the novelist, sincerity here feels a need of the signs of falsehood, and of conspicuous falsehood in order to last and to be consumed. Writing is the product, and ultimately the source, of this ambiguity. This specialized language, the use of which gives the writer a glorious but none the less superintended function, evinces a kind of servitude, invisible at first, which characterizes any responsibility. Writing, free in its beginnings, is finally the bond which links the writer to a History which is itself in chains : society stamps upon him the unmistakable signs of art so as to draw him along the more inescapably in its own process of alienation.

* *Larvatus prodeo* was the motto of Descartes.

IS THERE ANY POETIC
WRITING?

In the classical period, prose and poetry are quantities, their difference can be measured; they are
neither more nor less separated than two different
numbers, contiguous like them, but dissimilar because
of the very difference in their magnitudes. If I use the
word prose for a minimal form of speech, the most
economical vehicle for thought, and if I use the letters a, b, c for certain attributes of language, which
are useless but decorative, such as metre, rhyme or the
ritual of images, all the linguistic surface will be
accounted for in M. Jourdain's* double equation :

$$\text{Poetry} = \text{Prose} + a + b + c$$
$$\text{Prose} = \text{Poetry} - a - b - c$$

whence it clearly follows that Poetry is always
different from Prose. But this difference is not one of
essence, it is one of quantity. It does not, therefore,
jeopardize the unity of language, which is an article of
classical dogma. One may effect a different dosage in
manner of speech, according to the social occasion :
here, prose or rhetoric, there, poetry or precosity, in

* Molière's *Bourgeois Gentilhomme*.

accordance with a whole ritual of expression laid down by good society, but there remains everywhere a single language, which reflects the eternal categories of the mind. Classical poetry is felt to be merely an ornamental variation of prose, the fruit of an *art* (that is, a technique), never a different language, or the product of a particular sensibility. Any poetry is then only the decorative equation, whether allusive or forced, of a possible prose which is latent, virtually and potentially, in any conceivable manner of expression. 'Poetic', in the days of classicism, never evokes any particular domain, any particular depth of feeling, any special coherence, or separate universe, but only an individual handling of a verbal technique, that of 'expressing oneself' according to rules more artistic, therefore more sociable, than those of conversation, in other terms, the technique of projecting out an inner thought, springing fully armed from the Mind, a speech which is made more socially acceptable by virtue of the very conspicuousness of its conventions.

We know that nothing of this structure remains in modern poetry, which springs not from Baudelaire but from Rimbaud, unless it is in cases where one takes up again, in a revised traditional mode, the formal imperatives of classical poetry: henceforth, poets give to their speech the status of a closed Nature, which covers both the function and the structure of language. Poetry is then no longer a Prose either ornamental or shorn of liberties. It is a quality *sui generis* and without antecedents. It is no longer an attribute but a substance, and therefore it can very well renounce signs, since it carries its own nature within itself, and does not need to signal its identity outwardly: poetic language and prosaic language are sufficiently separate to be able to dispense with the very signs of their difference.

Furthermore, the alleged relations between thought and language are reversed; in classical art, a ready-made thought generates an utterance which 'expresses' or 'translates' it. Classical thought is devoid of duration, classical poetry has it only in such degree as is necessary to its technical arrangement. In modern poetics, on the contrary, words produce a kind of formal continuum from which there gradually emanates an intellectual or emotional density which would have been impossible without them; speech is then the solidified time of a more spiritual gestation, during which the 'thought' is prepared, installed little by little by the contingency of words. This verbal luck, which will bring down the ripe fruit of a meaning, presupposes therefore a poetic time which is no longer that of a 'fabrication', but that of a possible adventure, the meeting-point of a sign and an intention. Modern poetry is opposed to classical art by a difference which involves the whole structure of language, without leaving between those two types of poetry anything in common except the same sociological intention.

The economy of classical language (Prose and Poetry) is relational, which means that in it words are abstracted as much as possible in the interest of relationships. In it, no word has a density by itself, it is hardly the sign of a thing, but rather the means of conveying a connection. Far from plunging into an inner reality consubstantial to its outer configuration, it extends, as soon as it is uttered, towards other words, so as to form a superficial chain of intentions. A glance at the language of mathematics will perhaps enable us to grasp the relational nature of classical prose and poetry: we know that in mathematical language, not only is each quantity provided with a sign, but also that the relations between these quantities are themselves transcribed, by means of a sign expressing operative equality or difference. It may be said that the whole movement of mathematical flow derives from an explicit reading of its relations. The language of classicism is animated by an analogous, although of course less rigid, movement: its 'words', neutralized, made absent by rigorous recourse to a tradition which dessicates their freshness, avoid the phonetic or semantic accident which would concentrate the flavour of language at one point and halt its intellectual momentum in the interest of an un-equally distributed enjoyment. The classical flow is a succession of elements whose density is even; it is exposed to the same emotional pressure, and relieves those elements of any tendency towards an individual meaning appearing at all invented. The poetic vocabulary itself is one of usage, not of invention: images in it are recognizable in a body; they do not exist in isolation; they are due to long custom, not to individual creation. The function of the classical poet is not therefore to find new words, with more body or more brilliance, but to follow the order of an ancient ritual, to perfect the symmetry or the conciseness of a relation, to bring a thought exactly within the compass of a metre. Classical conceits involve relations, not words: they belong to an art of expression, not of invention. The words, here, do not, as they later do, thanks to a kind of violent and unexpected abruptness, reproduce the depth and singularity of an individual experience; they are spread out to form a surface, according to the exigencies of an elegant or decorative purpose. They delight us because of the formulation which brings them together, not because of their own power or beauty.

True, classical language does not reach the functional perfection of the relational network of mathematics: relations are not signified, in it, by any special signs, but only by accidents of form and disposition. It is the restraint of the words in itself, their alignment, which achieves the relational nature of classical discourse. Overworked in a restricted number of ever-similar relations, classical words are on the way to becoming an algebra where rhetorical figures of speech, clichés, function as virtual linking devices; they have lost their density and gained a more interrelated state of speech; they operate in the manner of chemical valences, outlining a verbal area full of symmetrical connections, junctions and net-works from which arise, without the respite afforded by wonder, fresh intentions towards signification. Hardly have the fragments of classical discourse yielded their meaning than they become messengers or harbingers, carrying ever further a meaning which refuses to settle within the depths of a word, but tries instead to spread widely enough to become a total gesture of intellection, that is, of communication.

Now the distortion to which Hugo tried to subject the alexandrine, which is of all meters the most inter-relational, already contains the whole future of modern poetry, since what is attempted is to elimin-ate the intention to establish relationships and to produce instead an explosion of words. For modern poetry, since it must be distinguished from classical poetry and from any type of prose, destroys the spontaneously functional nature of language, and leaves standing only its lexical basis. It retains only the outward shape of relationships, their music, but not their reality. The Word shines forth above a line

"outward shape of relationships" - interplay of signifiers
"reality" - the signified

of relationships emptied of their content, grammar is bereft of its purpose, it becomes prosody and is no longer anything but an inflexion which lasts only to present the Word. Connections are not properly speaking abolished, they are merely reserved areas, a parody of themselves, and this void is necessary for the density of the Word to rise out of a magic vacuum, like a sound and a sign devoid of background, like 'fury and mystery'.

In classical speech, connections lead the word on, and at once carry it towards a meaning which is an ever-deferred project; in modern poetry, connections are only an extension of the word, it is the Word which is 'the dwelling place', it is rooted like a *fons et origo* in the prosody of functions, which are perceived but unreal. Here, connections only fascinate, and it is the Word which gratifies and fulfills like the sudden revelation of a truth. To say that this truth is of a poetic order is merely to say that the Word in poetry can never be untrue, because it is a whole; it shines with an infinite freedom and prepares to radiate towards innumerable uncertain and possible connections. Fixed connections being abolished, the word is left only with a vertical project, it is like a monolith, or a pillar which plunges into a totality of meanings, reflexes and recollections: it is a sign which stands. The poetic word is here an act without immediate past, without environment, and which holds forth only the dense shadow of reflexes from all sources which are associated with it. Thus under each Word in modern poetry there lies a sort of existential geology, in which is gathered the total content of the Name, instead of a chosen content as in classical prose and poetry. The Word is no longer guided *in advance* by the general intention of a socialized discourse; the consumer of poetry, deprived of the guide of selective connections, encounters the Word frontally, and receives it as an absolute quantity, accompanied by all its possible associations. The Word, here, is encyclopaedic, it contains simultaneously all the acceptations from which a relational discourse might have required it to choose. It therefore achieves a state which is possible only in the dictionary or in poetry – places where the noun can live without its article – and is reduced to a sort of zero degree, pregnant with all past and future specifications. The word here has a generic form; it is a category. Each poetic word is thus an unexpected object, a Pandora's box from which fly out all the potentialities of language; it is therefore produced and consumed with a peculiar curiosity, a kind of sacred relish. This Hunger of the Word, common to the whole of modern poetry, makes poetic speech terrible and inhuman. It initiates a discourse full of gaps and full of lights, filled with absences and over-nourishing signs, without foresight or stability of intention, and thereby so opposed to the social function of language that merely to have recourse to a discontinuous speech is to open the door to all that stands above Nature.

For what does the rational economy of classical language mean, if not that Nature is a plenum, that it can be possessed, that it does not shy away or cover itself in shadows, but is in its entirety subjected to the toils of language? Classical language is always reducible to a persuasive continuum, it postulates the possibility of dialogue, it establishes a universe in which men are not alone, where words never have the terrible weight of things, where speech is always a meeting with the others. Classical language is a bringer of euphoria because it is immediately social. There is no genre, no written work of classicism which does not suppose a collective consumption, akin to speech; classical literary art is an object which circulates among several persons brought together on a class basis; it is a product conceived for oral transmission, for a consumption regulated by the contingencies of society: it is essentially a spoken language, in spite of its strict codification.

We have seen that on the contrary modern poetry destroyed relationships in language and reduced discourse to words as static things. This implies a reversal in our knowledge of Nature. The interrupted flow of the new poetic language initiates a discontinuous Nature, which is revealed only piecemeal. At the very moment when the withdrawal of functions obscures the relations existing in the world, the object in discourse assumes an exalted place : modern poetry is a poetry of the object. In it, Nature becomes a fragmented space, made of objects solitary and terrible, because the links between them are only potential. Nobody chooses for them a privileged meaning, or a particular use, or some service; nobody imposes a hierarchy on them, nobody reduces them to the manifestation of a mental behaviour, or of an intention, of some evidence of tenderness, in short. The bursting upon us of the poetic word then institutes an absolute object; Nature becomes a succession of verticalities, of objects, suddenly standing erect, and filled with all their possibilities : one of these can be only a landmark in an unfulfilled, and thereby terrible, world. These unrelated objects – words adorned with all the violence of their irruption, the vibration of which, though wholly mechanical, strangely affects the next word, only to die out immediately – these poetic words exclude men : there is no humanism of modern poetry. This erect discourse is full of terror, that is to say, it relates man not to other men, but to the most inhuman images in Nature : heaven, hell, holiness, childhood, madness, pure matter, etc.

At such a point, it is hardly possible to speak of a poetic mode of writing, for this is a language in which a violent drive towards autonomy destroys any ethical scope. The verbal gesture here aims at modifying Nature, it is the approach of a demiurge; it is not an attitude of the conscience but an act of coercion. Such, at least, is the language of those modern poets who carry their intention to the limit, and assume Poetry not as a spiritual exercise, a state of the soul or a placing of oneself in a situation, but as the splendour and freshness of a dream language. For such poets, it is as vain to speak about a mode of writing as of poetic feeling. Modern Poetry, in Char, for instance, is beyond this diffuse tone, this precious *aura*, which *are*, indeed, a mode of writing, usually termed poetic feeling. There is no objection to speaking of a poetic mode of writing concerning the classical writers and their epigones, or even concerning poetic prose in the manner of Gide's *Fruits of the Earth*, in which Poetry is in fact a certain linguistic ethos. In both cases, the mode of writing soaks up the style, and we can imagine that for people living in the seventeenth century, it was not easy to perceive an *immediate* difference between Racine and Pradon (and even less a difference of a poetic kind), just as it is not easy for a modern reader to pass judgment on those contemporary poets who use the same uniform and indecisive poetic mode of writing, because for them Poetry is a *climate* which means, essentially, a linguistic convention. But when the poetic language radically questions Nature by virtue of its very structure, without any resort to the content of the discourse and without falling back on some ideology, there is no mode of writing left, there are only styles, thanks to which man turns his back on society and confronts the world of objects without going through any of the forms of History or of social life.

Part Two

THE TRIUMPH AND BREAK-UP OF BOURGEOIS WRITING

There is, in pre-classical Literature, the appearance of a variety of modes of writing; but this variety seems far less wide if one puts these linguistic problems in terms of structure and not in terms of art. Aesthetically, the sixteenth and the beginning of the seventeenth centuries show a fairly lavish profusion of literary languages because men are still engaged in the task of getting to know Nature, and not yet in that of giving expression to man's essence. On these grounds, the encyclopaedic writing of Rabelais, or the precious writing of Corneille – to take only such typical moments – have as a common form a language in which ornaments are not yet ritualistic but are in themselves a method of investigation applied to the whole surface of the world. This is what gives to this pre-classical writing the genuine appearance of many-sidedness, and the euphoria which comes from freedom. For a modern reader, the impression of variety is all the stronger since the French tongue seems to be still experimenting with unstable structures, and since it has not yet fully settled on the character of its syntax or the laws governing the increase of its vocabulary. To take up again the distinction between a language and a mode of writing, we can say that until around 1650, French literature had not yet gone further than the problematics of the language, and that by this very fact, it was as yet unaware of modes of writing. For as long as a tongue is still uncertain about its very structure, an ethics of language is impossible; modes of writing appear only when the language, being established on a national scale, becomes a kind of negativity, a line which separates what is forbidden from what is allowed, without asking itself any more questions about its origins or the justifications for such a taboo. By creating an intemporal reason working through the language, the classical grammarians have relieved the French from any linguistic problem, and this purified language has become a mode of writing, that is, a language to which is attached a value, and which is given immediately as universal by very virtue of the historical situation.

The diversity of the 'genres' and the varying rhythms of styles within the framework of classical dogma are aesthetic, not structural, data; neither must deceive us : there was indeed one and only one mode of writing, both instrumental and ornamental, at the disposal of French society during the whole period when bourgeois ideology conquered and triumphed. Instrumental, since form was supposed to be at the service of content, just as an algebraic equation is at the service of an operational process; ornamental, since the instrument in question was embellished with accidental features external to its function, and unselfconsciously borrowed from Tradition, so that this bourgeois mode of writing, taken in turn by different writers, was never shunned for its pedigree, since it was only a felicitous backcloth against which the act of thought was thrown into relief. Classical writers have indeed themselves faced problems of form, but the point at issue was in no way the plurality and meaning of modes of writing, still less the structure of the language. The only thing in question was rhetoric, namely the ordering of discourse in such a way as to persuade. To a single bourgeois writing there corresponded, therefore, several rhetorics; conversely, it was at the very moment when treatises on rhetoric aroused no more interest, towards the middle of the nineteenth century, that classical writing ceased to be universal and that modern modes of writing came into being.

This classical writing is, needless to say, a class writing. Born in the seventeeth century in the group which was closest to the people in power, shaped by force of dogmatic decisions, promptly ridding itself of all grammatical turns of speech forged by the spontaneous subjectivity of ordinary people, and drilled, on the contrary, for a task of definition, bourgeois writing was first presented, with the cynicism customary in the first flush of political victory, as the language of a privileged minority. In 1647, Vaugelas recommends classical writing as a *de facto*, not a *de jure*, state of affairs; clear expression is still only court usage. In 1660, on the contrary, in the *Grammaire* of Port-Royal for instance, classical language wears a universal look, and clarity has become a value. In actual fact, clarity is a purely rhetorical attribute, not a quality of language in general, which is possible at all times and in all places, but only the ideal appendage to a certain type of discourse, that which is given over to a permanent intention to persuade. It is because the pre-bourgeoisie of the *Ancien Régime* and the post-revolutionary bourgeoisie, using the same mode of writing, have developed an essentialist mythology of man, that classical writing, unified and universal, renounced all hesitancy in favour of a continuum in which every fragment was a *choice*, that is, the radical elimination of all virtualities in language. Political authority, spiritualistic dogmatism, and unity in the language of classicism are therefore various aspects of the same historical movement.

So it is no wonder that the Revolution changed nothing in bourgeois writing, and that there is only a slight difference between the writing of, say, Fénelon and Mérimée. This is because bourgeois ideology remained intact until 1848 without being in the least shaken by a Revolution which gave the bourgeoisie

political and social power, although not the intellectual power, which it had long held. From Laclos to
Stendhal, bourgeois writing needed only to resume its
continuity after the short interruption of troubled
times. And the romantic revolution, so theoretically
committed to the overthrow of traditional forms, in
the event, stuck prudently to the writing of its ideology. A few concessions such as the mixing of genres
and words enabled it to preserve the main feature of
classical language, namely, instrumentality. True, this
instrument comes more and more to the fore (notably
in Chateaubriand), but all in all it is still an instrument, used without aloofness, and not yet, as a language, conscious of solitude. Hugo alone, by evolving,
out of the concrete dimensions of his own personal
time and space, a particular and thematic use of language, which could no longer be understood with
reference to a tradition, but only in the light of the
formidable reality lying behind his own existence,
Hugo alone, then, through the weight of his style,
was able to exert some pressure on classical writing
and bring it to the verge of disintegration. This is
why contempt for Hugo still serves to bolster up the
self-same writing in eighteenth century taste, which
witnessed the heyday of the bourgeoisie, and remains
the norm of 'accepted' French, a carefully closed language, separated from society by the whole body of
the literary myth, a consecrated mode of writing used
indiscriminately by the most heterogeneous writers as

an austere duty or a connoisseur's relish, a tabernacle of this awe-inspiring mystery: French Literature.

Now the 1850s bring the concurrence of three new and important facts in History: the demographic expansion in Europe, the replacement of textile by heavy industry, that is, the birth of modern capitalism, the scission (completed by the revolution of June 1848) of French society into three mutually hostile classes, bringing the definitive ruin of liberal illusions. These circumstances put the bourgeoisie into a new historical situation. Until then, it was bourgeois ideology itself which gave the measure of the universal by fulfilling it unchallenged. The bourgeois writer, sole judge of other people's woes and without anyone else to gaze on him, was not torn between his social condition and his intellectual vocation. Henceforth, this very ideology appears merely as one among many possible others; the universal escapes it, since transcending itself would mean condemning itself; the writer falls a prey to ambiguity, since his consciousness no longer accounts for the whole of his condition. Thus is born a tragic predicament peculiar to Literature.

It is at this moment that modes of writing begin to multiply. Each one, henceforth, be it the highly wrought, populist, neutral or colloquial, sets itself up as the initial act whereby the writer acknowledges or repudiates his bourgeois condition. Each one is an attempt to find a solution to this Orphean problematics of modern Form: writers without Literature. For the last hundred years, Flaubert, Mallarmé, Rimbaud, the Goncourt brothers, the Surrealists, Queneau, Sartre, Blanchot or Camus, have outlined – indeed are still outlining – certain ways of integrating, disrupting or naturalizing literary language; but what is at stake is not some adventure of literary form, some success in rhetorical achievement or some bold use of vocabulary. Whenever the writer assembles a network of words it is the existence of Literature itself which is called into question; what modernity allows us to read in the plurality of modes of writing, is the blind alley which is its own History.

STYLE AS CRAFTSMANSHIP

'Form is costly,' Valéry would answer when asked why he did not publish his lectures at the Collège de France. Yet there has been a whole period, that of triumphant bourgeois writing, when form cost about the same price as thought. It is true that attention was paid to its conciseness and order, and to its euphemistic grace, but form was all the cheaper since the writer was using a ready-made instrument, the working of which was handed down unchanged without anyone being obsessed with novelty. Form was not seen as a possession; the universality of classical language derived from the fact that language was common property, and that thought alone bore the weight of being different. We might say that throughout this period, form had a usage value.

Now we have seen that around 1850, Literature begins to face a problem of self-justification; it is now on the point of seeking alibis for itself; and precisely because the shadow of a doubt begins to be cast on its usage, a whole class of writers anxious to assume to the full the responsibility of their tradition is about to put the work-value of writing in place of its usage-value. Writing is now to be saved not by virtue of what it exists for, but thanks to the work it has cost. There begins now to grow up an image of the writer as a craftsman who shuts himself away in some legendary place, like a workman operating at home, and who roughs out, cuts, polishes and sets his form exactly as a jeweller extracts art from his material, devoting to his work regular hours of solitary effort. Writers like Gautier (past master in Belles-Lettres), Flaubert (grinding away at his sentences at Croisset), Valéry (in his room at the crack of dawn) or Gide (standing at his desk like a carpenter at his bench) form a kind of guild of French Literature, in which work expended on form is the sign and the property of a corporation. Labour replaces genius as a value, so to speak; there is a kind of ostentation in claiming to labour long and lovingly over the form of one's work. There even arises, sometimes, a preciosity of conciseness (for labouring at one's material usually means reducing it), in contrast to the great preciosity of the baroque era (that of Corneille, for instance). For the latter expresses a knowledge of Nature which necessitates a broadening of the language; but the former, trying to evolve an aristocratic literary style, lays down the conditions for a historical crisis, destined to begin on the day when an aesthetic aim no longer suffices to justify the convention which this anachronistic language represents, that is, on the day when History has brought about an obvious disjunction between the social vocation of the writer and the instrument which he has inherited from Tradition.

Flaubert it was who most methodically laid the foundations for this conception of writing as craft. Before him, the existence of the bourgeois was a picturesque or exotic phenomenon; bourgeois ideology supplied the norm of the universal and, postulating that pure man existed as such, could experience a sense of well-being as it contemplated the bourgeois as a spectacle in no way commensurate with itself. Whereas for Flaubert the bourgeois state is an incurable ill which sticks to the writer, and which he can cure only by assuming it clear-sightedly – which is of the essence of tragic feeling. This bourgeois Necessity which characterizes Frédéric Moreau, Emma Bovary, Bouvard and Pécuchet, requires, as soon as it is squarely faced and accepted, an art which is equally the bearer of a necessity, and armed with a Law. Flaubert founded a normative writing which – and this is a paradox – includes technical rules which can reveal pathos. On the one hand, he builds his narrative by a succession of essences, and not at all by following a phenomenological order (as Proust later does); he finalizes the uses of verbal tenses according to a convention, so as to make them perform the function of *signs* of Literature, in the manner of an art drawing attention to its very artificiality; he elaborates a rhythm of the written word which creates a sort of incantation and which, quite unlike the rules of spoken eloquence, appeals to a sixth, purely literary, sense, the private property of producers and consumers of Literature. And on the other hand this code of literary labour, this sum of exercises related to the writer's work, keep up a wisdom, so to speak, which is also touched with sadness, and openness too, since the art of Flaubert points to its mask as it moves forward. What this Gregorian codification of literary language aimed at was, if not the reconciliation of the writer to a universal condition, at least the conferment upon him of the responsibility for his form, the transmutation of the writing handed down to him by History into an *art;* in other words, into an obvious convention, a sincere pact which would enable man to adopt a position he was familiar with in a nature still made of ill-matched realities. The writer then gives to society a self-confessed art, whose rules are visible to all, and in exchange society is able to accept the writer. Baudelaire, for instance, insisted on tracing the admirable prosaicness of his poetry back to Gautier, to a kind of fetish of *highly wrought* form, situated no doubt outside pragmatic bourgeois activity, but inserted into an order of familiar tasks, under the eye of a society which recognized in it not its dreams but its methods. Since Literature could not be vanquished by its own weapons, was it not better to accept it openly, and, being condemned to this literary hard labour, to 'do good work' in it? So the 'Flaubertization' of writing redeems all writers at a stroke, partly because the least exacting abandon themselves to it without qualms, and partly because the purest return to it as to an acknowledgment of their fate.

naive devices of his school, whereby the natural sentence is transformed into an artificial one meant to bear witness to its purely literary purpose, which means, in this instance, to what it cost in labour. We know that according to Maupassant's stylistics, the artistic intention is the preserve of syntax, the vocabulary being meant to stay on this side of Literature. To write well – now the sole sign of literary reality – means naively to shift the place of a predicate, to 'set off' a word while being hopeful of obtaining by this means an 'expressive' rhythm. But expressiveness is a myth: it is only the convention of expressiveness.

This conventional mode of writing has always been a happy hunting ground for study in schools, where the value of a text is assessed by the obvious signs of the labour it has cost. Now nothing is more spectacular than attempting to combine predicates, as a workman adjusts some delicate mechanism. What pedants admire in the writing of a Maupassant or a Daudet is a literary sign at last detached from its content, which posits Literature unambiguously as a category without any relation to other languages, and in so doing establishes an ideal intelligibility of things. Between a proletariat excluded from all culture, and an intelligentsia which has already begun to question Literature itself, the average public produced by primary and secondary schools, namely lower-middle class, roughly speaking, will therefore

[handwritten margin notes:] "predicate" "a complement to the structure" –Jakobson (metonymy)

[handwritten margin note:] – but not from its significant –

[handwritten note at bottom of page:] this "ideal intelligibility" is the intelligibility championed by the new critics – a literature that knows how to talk about the things worth talking about in the "code for those" – a code for "play."

find in the artistic-realistic mode of writing – which is that of a good proportion of commercial novels – the image *par excellence* of a Literature which has all the striking and intelligible signs of its identity. In this case the function of the writer is not so much to create a work as to supply a Literature which can be seen from afar.

This lower-middle-class mode of writing has been taken up by communist writers because, for the time being, the artistic norms of the proletariat cannot be different from those of the *petite bourgeoisie* (a fact which indeed agrees with their doctrine), and because the very dogma of socialist realism necessarily entails the adoption of a conventional mode of writing, to which is assigned the task of signifying in a conspicuous way a content which is powerless to impose itself without a form to identify it. Thus is understood the paradox whereby the communist mode of writing makes multiple use of the grossest signs of Literature, and far from breaking with a form which is after all typically bourgeois – or which was such in the past, at least – goes on assuming without reservation the formal preoccupations of the *petit-bourgeois* art of writing (which is moreover accredited with the communist public, thanks to the essays done in the primary school).

70

French socialist realism has therefore taken up the mode of writing of bourgeois realism, mechanizing without restraint all the intentional signs of art. Here are for instance a few lines of a novel by Garaudy: ' … with torso bent, he launched himself at full speed on the keyboard of the linotype … joy sang in his muscles, his fingers danced, light and powerful … the poisoned vapour of antimony … made his temples pulsate and his arteries hammer, fanning his strength, his anger and his mental exaltation.' We see that nothing here is given without metaphor, for it must be laboriously borne home to the reader that 'it is well written' (that is, that what he is consuming is Literature). These metaphors, which seize the very slightest verb, in no way indicate the intention of an individual Humour trying to convey the singularity of a sensation, but only a literary stamp which 'places' a language, just as a label tells us the price of an article.

'To type', 'to throb' or 'to be happy for the first time', is real, not Realist language; for Literature to come into existence one must write: 'to strum on the linotype', 'his arteries hammered …' or 'he was clutching the first happy moment of his life.' Realist writing can therefore lead only to a species of preciosity. Garaudy writes: 'At the end of each line, the thin arm of the linotype plucked away a handful of dancing matrices,' or 'Each caress of his fingers awakes and sends a shiver through the joyous chime of copper matrices which fall into the grooves in a tinkling shower of notes.' This jargon is really no different from that of Cathos and Magdelon.*

Of course, we must allow for mediocrity; in the case of Garaudy, it is impressive. In André Stil, we shall find devices which are much more discreet but which do not escape the rules of artistic-realist writing. Here metaphors do not pretend to be more than a cliché, almost fully integrated to real language, and signifying Literature at no great cost : 'crystal clear', 'hands white as parchment with the cold', etc. The preciosity is driven from the vocabulary into the syntax, and it is the artificial arrangement of the predicates, as in Maupassant, which establishes the text as Literature ('with one hand, she lifts up the knees, her body bent'). This language, steeped in conventionality, presents reality only in inverted commas : would-be working-class words, slipshod turns of speech are used together with a purely literary syntax : 'That's true, it's kicking up a shindy all right, that wind!', or even better : 'Their bérets and caps buffeted in the wind above their eyes, they look at each other pretty quizzically' (in which the colloquial 'pretty' follows an absolute participle, a form of speech totally unknown in spoken language). Needless to say, one must set Aragon in a class apart, since his literary antecedents are of a quite different kind, and since he has preferred to mix in with realist writing a slight

* Cathos and Magdelon are Molière's *Précieuses Ridicules*.

eighteenth century colour, adding a little Laclos to
Zola.

Perhaps there is, in this well-behaved writing of
revolutionaries, a feeling of powerlessness to create
forthwith a free writing. Perhaps also the fact that
only bourgeois writers can feel that bourgeois writing
is compromised: the disintegration of literary language was a phenomenon which owed its existence
to consciousness, not to revolution. And certainly the
fact that Stalinist ideology imposes a terror before all
problematics, even and above all revolutionary:
bourgeois writing is thought to be all in all less
dangerous than its being put on trial. This is why
communist writers are the only ones who go on im-
perturbably keeping alive a bourgeois writing which
bourgeois writers have themselves condemned long
ago, since the day when they felt it was endangered
by the impostures of their own ideology, namely, the
day when Marxism was thereby justified.

WRITING AND SILENCE

Craftsmanlike writing, since it lies within the bourgeois heritage, does not disturb any order; although deprived of other battles, the writer retains a passion which provides him with sufficient justification: the bringing forth of form. If he renounces the task of setting free a new literary language, he can at least enhance the existing one with new intentions, conceits, purple patches or archaisms, and create another, which is rich and mortal. This great traditional writing, that of Gide, Valéry, Montherlant, even Breton, means that form, through the weight of its unusual posturing, is a value which transcends History, in the same way as a ritual language of priests.

Other writers have thought that they could exorcize this sacred writing only by dislocating it. They have therefore undermined literary language, they have ceaselessly exploded the ever-renewed husk of clichés, of habits, of the formal past of the writer; in a chaos of forms and a wilderness of words they hoped they would achieve an object wholly delivered of History, and find again the freshness of a pristine state of language. But such upheavals end up by leaving their own tracks and creating their own laws. The threat of becoming a Fine Art is a fate which hangs over any language not based exclusively on the speech of society. In a perpetual flight forward from a disorderly syntax, the disintegration of language can only lead to the silence of writing. The final agraphia of Rimbaud or of some Surrealists (who *ipso facto* fell into oblivion), this poignant self-destruction of Literature, teaches us that for some writers, language, the first and last way out of the literary myth, finally restores what it had hoped to avoid, that there is no writing which can be lastingly revolutionary, and that any silence of form can escape imposture only by complete abandonment of communication. Mallarmé, the Hamlet of writing, as it were, well represents this precarious moment of History in which literary language persists only the better to sing the necessity of its death. Mallarmé's typographical agraphia seeks to create around rarefied words an empty zone in which speech, liberated from its guilty social overtones, may, by some happy contrivance, no longer reverberate. The word, dissociated from the husk of habitual clichés, and from the technical reflexes of the writer, is then freed from responsibility in relation to all possible context; it appears in one brief act, which, being devoid of reflections, declares its solitude, and therefore its innocence. This art has the very structure of suicide: in it, silence is a homogeneous poetic time which traps the

word between two layers and sets it off less as a fragment of a cryptogram than as a light, a void, a
murder, a freedom. (We know all that this hypothesis
of Mallarmé as a murderer of language owes to
Maurice Blanchot.) This language of Mallarmé's is
like Orpheus who can save what he loves only by
renouncing it, and who, just the same, cannot resist
glancing round a little; it is Literature brought to the
gates of the Promised Land : a world without Literature, but one to which writers would nevertheless
have to bear witness.

In this same attempt towards disengaging literary
language, here is another solution : to create a colourless writing, freed from all bondage to a pre-ordained
state of language. A simile borrowed from linguistics
will perhaps give a fairly accurate idea of this new
phenomenon; we know that some linguists establish
between the two terms of a polar opposition (such as
singular-plural, preterite-present) the existence of a
third term, called a neutral term or zero element :
thus between the subjunctive and the imperative
moods, the indicative is according to them an amodal
form. Proportionately speaking, writing at the zero
degree is basically in the indicative mood, or if you
like, amodal; it would be accurate to say that it is a
journalist's writing, if it were not precisely the case

that journalism develops, in general, optative or imperative (that is, emotive) forms. The new neutral writing takes its place in the midst of all those ejaculations and judgments, without becoming involved in any of them; it consists precisely in their absence. But this absence is complete, it implies no refuge, no secret; one cannot therefore say that it is an impassive mode of writing; rather, that it is innocent. The aim here is to go beyond Literature by entrusting one's fate to a sort of basic speech, equally far from living languages and from literary language proper. This transparent form of speech, initiated by Camus's *Outsider*, achieves a style of absence which is almost an ideal absence of style; writing is then reduced to a sort of negative mood in which the social or mythical characters of a language are abolished in favour of a neutral and inert state of form; thus thought remains wholly responsible, without being overlaid by a secondary commitment of form to a History not its own. If Flaubert's writing enshrines a Law, if that of Mallarmé postulates a silence, and if others, those of Proust, Céline, Queneau, Prévert, each in its own way, is founded on the existence of a social nature, if all these modes of writing imply an opacity of form and presuppose a problematic of language and society, thus establishing speech as an object which must receive treatment at the hands of a craftsman, a magician or a scriptor, but not by an intellectual, then neutral writing in fact rediscovers the primary condition of classical art: instrumentality. But this time, form as an instrument is no longer at the service of a triumphant ideology; it is the mode of a new situation of the writer, the way a certain silence has of existing; it deliberately forgoes any elegance or ornament, for these two dimensions would reintroduce Time into writing, and this is a derivative power which sustains History. If the writing is really neutral, and if language, instead of being a cumbersome and recalcitrant act, reaches the state of a pure equation, which is no more tangible than an algebra when it confronts the innermost part of man, then Literature is vanquished, the problematics of mankind is uncovered and presented without elaboration, the writer becomes irretrievably honest. Unfortunately, nothing is more fickle than a colourless writing; mechanical habits are developed in the very place where freedom existed, a network of set forms hem in more and more the pristine freshness of discourse, a mode of writing appears afresh in lieu of an indefinite language. The writer, taking his place as a 'classic', becomes the slavish imitator of his original creation, society demotes his writing to a mere manner, and returns him a prisoner to his own formal myths.

WRITING AND SPEECH

A little more than a hundred years ago, writers were for the most part unaware that there were several ways – and very different ones – of speaking French. Around 1830, at the time when the bourgeoisie found good-humoured entertainment in everything situated on the fringe of its own preserve, namely in that inconsiderable portion of society which it was willing to share with bohemians, concierges and pickpockets, there began to find their way into literary language proper a few extraneous scraps lifted from inferior forms of language, provided they were suitably eccentric (otherwise they would have been a source of danger). These picturesque jargons embellished Literature without threatening its structure. Balzac, Süe, Monnier, Hugo found enjoyment in reinstating a few really aberrant forms of pronunciation and vocabulary: thieves' argot, country dialects, German jargon, or the lingo of the concierges. But this social speech, which was a kind of theatrical costume hung on to an essence, never involved the speaker as a total person; the mechanism of the passions went on functioning over and above the speech.

It was perhaps necessary to wait for Proust to see the writer fuse certain men totally with their language, and present his creatures only through that solid and colourful guise, their way of speaking. While Balzac's creatures, for instance, are easily reducible to the power relations of the society of which they are, so to speak, the algebraic expressions, a character of Proust materializes into the opacity of a particular language, and it is really at this level that his whole historical situation – his profession, his class, his wealth, his heredity, his bodily frame – is integrated and ordered. In this way, Literature begins to know society as a Nature, the phenomena of which it might perhaps be able to reproduce. During such moments when the writer follows languages which are really spoken, no longer for the sake of picturesqueness, but as essential objects which fully account for the whole content of society, writing takes as the locus of its reflexes the real speech of men. Literature no longer implies pride or escape, it begins to become a lucid act of giving information; as if it had first to learn the particulars of social differences by reproducing them. It takes it upon itself to give an immediate account, as a preliminary to any other message, of the situation of men immured by the language of their class, their region, their profession, their heredity or their history.

Understood in this way, literary language founded on social speech never gets rid of a descriptive virtue

which limits it, since the universality of a language –
in the present state of society – is a fact concerning
hearing, and not speaking. Within a national norm
such as French, forms of expression differ in different
groups, and every man is a prisoner of his language:
outside his class, the first word he speaks is a sign
which places him as a whole and proclaims his whole
personal history. The man is put on show and delivered up by his language, betrayed by a formal
reality which is beyond the reach of his lies, whether
they are inspired by self-interest or generosity. The
diversity of languages therefore works like Necessity,
and it is because of this that it gives rise to a form of
the tragic.

So the restoration of spoken language, first invented in the playful mimicry of the picturesque,
ended by expressing the whole content of social con-
tradiction. In Céline's work, for instance, writing is
not at the service of thought, like some successfully
realistic décor tacked on to the description of a social
sub-class; it really represents the writer's descent into
the sticky opacity of the condition which he is de-
scribing. True, this is still a way of *expressing* it, and
Literature has not been left behind. But it must be
agreed that, among all the means of *description* (since
until now Literature has above all aimed at that), the

adoption of a real language is for the writer the most human act. And a sizable part of modern Literature is pervaded by the more or less elaborate shreds of this dream: a literary language which might emulate the naturalness of social languages. (We have only to think of the dialogues in Sartre's novels to give a recent and well-known example.) But however successful these pictures may be, they can never be any more than reproductions, arias, so to speak, surrounded by long recitatives in an entirely conventional mode of writing.

Queneau has tried, precisely, to show that it was possible to contaminate all the parts of the written discourse by spoken speech, and in his works the socialization of literary language takes a simultaneous hold on all the layers of writing: the spelling, the vocabulary, and – which is more important although less spectacular – the pace. Of course, this writing of Queneau's is not situated outside Literature, since it is still consumed by a limited section of society; it is not the vehicle of a universality, but only of an experiment and an entertainment. At least, for the first time, it is not the writing which is literary; Literature is expelled from Form and is now nothing but a category. Here, it is Literature which is irony, and language which is experienced in depth. Or rather, Literature is openly reduced to the problematics of language; and indeed, that is all it can now be.

We can see taking shape, by this means, the possible area of a new humanism : the general suspicion which has gradually overtaken language throughout modern literature gives way to a reconciliation between the logos of the writer and that of men. Only then can the writer declare himself entirely committed, when his poetic freedom takes its place within a verbal condition whose limits are those of society and not those of a convention or a public. Otherwise, commitment will always be purely nominal; it will be able to effect the salvation of one conscience, but not to provide a basis for action. It is because there is no thought without language, that Form is the first and last arbiter of literary responsibility, and it is because there is no reconciliation within the present society, that language, necessary and necessarily orientated, creates for the writer a situation fraught with conflict.

THE UTOPIA OF LANGUAGE

The multiplication of modes of writing is a modern phenomenon which forces a choice upon the writer, making form a kind of behaviour and giving rise to an ethic of writing. To all the dimensions which together made up the literary creation is henceforth added a new depth, since form is by itself a kind of parasitical mechanism of the intellectual function. Modern writing is a truly independent organism which grows around the literary act, decorates it with a value which is foreign to its intention, ceaselessly commits it to a double mode of existence, and superimposes upon the content of the words opaque signs which carry with them a history, a second-order meaning which compromises or redeems it, so that with the situation of thought is mingled a supplementary fate, often diverging from the former and always an encumbrance to it – the fate of the form.

Now this fatal character of the literary sign, which makes a writer unable to pen a word without taking a pose characteristic of an out-of-date, anarchic or imitative language – one in any case conventionalized and dehumanized – has taken effect precisely at the moment when Literature, abolishing more and more its condition as a bourgeois myth, is required as a document or a testimony of a humanism which has at last integrated History into its image of man. So that the old literary categories, emptied in the best instances of their traditional content, which was the expression of an intemporal essence of man, eventually stand only by virtue of a specific form, an order due to the vocabulary or the syntax, in short, quite simply a language: it is now writing which absorbs the whole identity of a literary work. A novel by Sartre is a novel only to the extent of its having remained faithful to a certain recitative tone, which is, moreover, intermittent, and whose norms have been established in the course of a whole previous geology of the novel: in fact, it is the mode of writing of the recitative, and not its content, which reintegrates the Sartrean novel into the category of Belles-Lettres. Furthermore, when Sartre attempts to break the time-flow typical of the novel, and duplicates his narrative in order to render the ubiquity of reality (in *The Reprieve*), it is the narrative mode of writing which recomposes, above the simultaneity of the events, a Time which is undivided and homogeneous, the Time of the Narrator, whose particular voice, defined by highly recognizable contingent features, burdens the unfolding of History with a parasitical unity, and gives the novel the ambiguity of a testimony which may well be false.

This shows that a modern masterpiece is impossible, since the writer is forced by his writing into a cleft stick : either the object of the work is naively attuned to the conventions of its form, Literature remaining deaf to our present History, and not going beyond the literary myth; or else the writer acknowledges the vast novelty of the present world, but finds that in order to express it he has at his disposal only a language which is splendid but lifeless. In front of the virgin sheet of paper, at the moment of choosing the words which must frankly signify his place in History, and testify that he assumes its data, he observes a tragic disparity between what he does and what he sees. Before his eyes, the world of society now exists as a veritable Nature, and this Nature speaks, elaborating living languages from which the writer is excluded : on the contrary, History puts in his hands a decorative and compromising instrument, a writing inherited from a previous and different History, for which he is not responsible and yet which is the only one he can use. Thus is born a tragic element in writing, since the conscious writer must henceforth fight against ancestral and all-powerful signs which, from the depths of a past foreign to him, impose Literature on him like some ritual, not like a reconciliation.

Therefore, unless they renounced Literature, the solution of this problematic of writing does not depend on the writer. Every writer born opens within himself the trial of literature, but if he condemns it, he always grants it a reprieve which literature turns to use in order to reconquer him. However hard he tries to create a free language, it comes back to him fabricated, for luxury is never innocent: and it is this stale language, closed by the immense pressure of all the men who do not speak it, which he must continue to use. Writing therefore is a blind alley, and it is because society itself is a blind alley. The writers of today feel this; for them, the search for a non-style or an oral style, for a zero level or a spoken level of writing is, all things considered, the anticipation of a homogeneous social state; most of them understand that there can be no universal language outside a concrete, and no longer a mystical or merely nominal, universality of society.

There is therefore in every present mode of writing a double postulation: there is the impetus of a break and the impetus of a coming to power, there is the very shape of every revolutionary situation, the fundamental ambiguity of which is that Revolution must of necessity borrow, from what it wants to destroy, the very image of what it wants to possess. Like modern art in its entirety, literary writing carries at the same time the alienation of History and the dream of History; as a Necessity, it testifies to the division of languages which is inseparable from the division of classes; as Freedom, it is the consciousness of this division and the very effort which seeks to surmount it. Feeling permanently guilty of its own solitude, it is none the less an imagination eagerly desiring a felicity of words, it hastens towards a dreamed-of language whose freshness, by a kind of ideal anticipation, might portray the perfection of some new Adamic world where language would no longer be alienated. The proliferation of modes of writing brings a new Literature into being in so far as the latter invents its language only in order to be a project: Literature becomes the Utopia of language.